100

THINGS TO DO IN
CHARLOTTESVILLE
BEFORE YOU
DIE

100

THINGS TO DO IN
CHARLOTTESVILLE
BEFORE YOU
DIE

3rd Edition

• •

MARIJEAN OLDHAM

REEDY PRESS

Library of Congress Control Number: 2021949228

ISBN: 9781681063546

Design by Jill Halpin

All photos by the author unless otherwise noted.

Printed in the United States of America
22 23 24 25 26   5 4 3 2 1

We (the publisher and the author) have done our best to provide the most accurate information available when this book was completed. However, we make no warranty, guarantee, or promise about the accuracy, completeness, or currency of the information provided, and we expressly disclaim all warranties, express or implied. Please note that attractions, company names, addresses, websites, and phone numbers are subject to change or closure, and this is outside of our control. We are not responsible for any loss, damage, injury, or inconvenience that may occur due to the use of this book. When exploring new destinations, please do your homework before you go. You are responsible for your own safety and health when using this book.

DEDICATION

To Seth, for proposing new things
to do every week, five at a time.

CONTENTS

• •

Music and Entertainment

Sports and Recreation

● ●

Culture and History

• •

Shopping and Fashion

• •

PREFACE

I fell hard for Charlottesville shortly after moving here at the end of 2005. Many others report the same kind of C'ville love, and in fact, people who first came to town as University of Virginia students often feel the call to return post-graduation. Central Virginia has a lot going for it that I like: wine, beautiful outdoor adventures, great food, smart people, social consciousness, and a lively arts scene. Charlottesville may be small, but it fits my personality like a glove.

The place that won me over on my first visit was the central highlight of the city: the Downtown Mall. No visit to Charlottesville is complete without a stroll on the pedestrian mall, a peek into the shops, a bite to eat at an outdoor restaurant, people watching, and busker-driven entertainment.

If the Downtown Mall is the center of Charlottesville, the radius extends for special occasions to nearby Staunton, Virginia, where the American Shakespeare Center has its home; to Shenandoah National Park for hiking and camping adventures; up north to Bowlero for a bowling date; or down south to the James River for a summertime tubing day. Part of the fun of this town is what's easily accessible, so get out and enjoy it!

Writing this book began as a relatively easy exercise. Ideas of what to do based on what I've done and what I hope to do just flowed onto the page. The challenge, of course, was whittling the list down to 100 and trying to fit the best of what's

• •

here on these pages—a formidable task, to be sure. Each recommendation was carefully considered and often personally investigated. The ideas keep coming, however, and with every season it seems exciting new things to do are available in this historic village. Plan a visit soon, and if you're a townie, get to work on crossing off items from your list of *100 Things to Do in Charlottesville Before You Die.*

ACKNOWLEDGMENTS

This is not the kind of book meant to be written, read, or experienced alone. A great many thanks go out to my six million (according to my dad) Facebook friends who shouted out great ideas. I've heard from folks intending to launch clubs designed to check off each recommended activity, and I'm eager to hear from those who do.

Special thanks to Seth Oldham, my husband and the cyclist who told me about the best route in the region. Thank you to my daughter, Allison Jaggers, whose late-night brainstorming sessions helped the list reach 100. Thank you to my son, Aaron Jaggers, for enthusiasm and a general sense of joy surrounding this project. Mountains of appreciation for Mary Sproles Martin, who keeps my hyphenating to a minimum and my capitalization in order. Last but not least, thank you to Amanda Doyle, who thought of me and of Charlottesville.

FOOD AND DRINK

MAKE A CHEESE PILGRIMAGE
TO THE MONASTERY IN WHITE HALL

Trust me on this: go to White Hall and buy some Gouda cheese, handmade by the nuns. The neighboring rural community of White Hall has only a couple of things going for it, but oh, are they worth it! First is a Trappist monastery, Our Lady of the Angels, populated and managed by a group of monastic nuns who, when they're not praying for our souls, make the most delicious cheese. Bring cash—a wheel of Gouda is $25 and worth every penny, as well as the scenic journey to get it.

If you like a little wine with your cheese, you're in luck. Pack some fruit, bread, and crackers to go with your cheese, and head to White Hall Winery for a perfect fall afternoon with friends.

Our Lady of the Angels Monastery
3365 Monastery Dr., Crozet, 434-823-1452
olamonastery.org

White Hall Vineyards
5282 Sugar Ridge Rd., Crozet, 434-823-8615
whitehallvineyards.com

PICK YOUR OWN FRUIT
FROM LOCAL ORCHARDS

We recommend peaches and strawberries from Chiles Orchard in Crozet in the summer and apples from Carter Mountain Orchard in the fall. Plan the trip to either orchard as an outing with the kids. Carter Mountain can be a long trip up the mountain in peak season with lots of other apple pickers, and conditions can be quite muddy. Step out of the orchard and into the Bold Rock Hard Cider tasting room on the premises, or stock up on apple butter, baked goods, crafts, and recipe books in the gift shop.

A visit to Chiles is a bit more straightforward, with a peach's time from tree to cashier to your car at a minimum, but stick around for a while and sample the fresh peach frozen custard before you head home to make your pies and cobblers.

Chiles Peach Orchard
1351 Greenwood Rd., Crozet, 434-823-1583
chilespeachorchard.com

Carter Mountain Orchard
1435 Carters Mountain Tr., 434-977-1833
cartermountainorchard.com

TRY GOURMET GELATO
IN SPLENDORA'S MANY FLAVORS

Splendora's is a small gelato shop surprising its guests with unexpected flavors and uncompromising quality. Across from the Regal Stonefield movie theater, Splendora's (sometimes referred to as Splendy's by locals) is the place for those seeking a high-quality frozen dessert experience. The gelato creator, owner Patricia Ross, likes to experiment with interesting flavors. Try the flavor flights, sometimes with themes, like the cocktail-inspired Don't be a Jerk flight that includes the following:

Paloma: Elvelo reposado tequila + grapefruit sorbet
Rum daiquiri: Plantation rum + lime sorbet
Laphroaig Earl Grey + maple lemon gelato
Campari + mandarin cream gelato
Ragged Branch cherry coffee + chipotle gelato

A flight is $10. Regular, everyday menu items and fan favorite flavors include amerena-amaretto, chocolate, coconut, gianduia-hazelnut-malaga-mango, pistachio raspberry, and stracciatella. It's the perfect way to cap off a movie date night or to sweeten up a Stonefield shopping trip.

2050 Bond St., #170, 757-408-0719

BE A NACHOVORE
AT BEER RUN

Before you die, you need to make multiple trips to Beer Run. One trip should be with a small group and include tasting several craft beers and consuming your weight in nachos. The nachos at Beer Run are my favorite nachos in the world.

Another trip should be for brunch on a Sunday. Order the best Bloody Mary with your meal, if you're so inclined, or perhaps a mimosa if you have a sweet tooth. The food is fantastic. They open at 11 a.m. and, no matter the time of year, are packed to the gills in short order, so get there early—or, at worst, right on time.

The third trip you make to Beer Run should be reflective. Sit at the bar and talk to the locals. Meet Bill. Browse the selection of beer to-go and take some with you. You'll recall the visits fondly, no matter how long it is between your previous visit and your next.

156 Carlton Rd., Ste. 203, 434-984-2337
beerrun.com

LEARN TO COOK
FROM CULINARY CONCEPTS AB

Take an in-person or virtual cooking class from one of the best around: Antwon Brinson. Brinson's business, Culinary Concepts AB, aims to help people make connections by learning to cook together. Select from one-on-one private cooking lessons with the chef himself; small, private classes with a group of friends (or ones you meet in class); or virtual classes in which you receive cooking instruction live while you work from the comfort of your own kitchen.

International recipes that explore flavor are a specialty of Brinson's classes. Creative, thought-provoking activities for students assist the Culinary Concepts mission: bringing people together through the creation of excellent dishes to be shared. Schedule a class for one or for a special group activity.

2041 Barracks Rd., 434-617-4545
culinaryconceptsab.com

CRUISE FOR BREWS
ALONG THE BREWERY TRAIL

The Know Good Beer Festival invites you to try two- or four-ounce samplings of regional and national beers, ciders, bourbons, and spirits at this extremely popular event. Annually in the spring, at IX Art Park, you can learn about brewing techniques, visit with other hops enthusiasts, eat local foods, and taste a wide variety of beers.

If the annual event isn't enough to wet your whistle (and really, how could it be?), there are several local breweries to visit. Our favorites? Champion Brewing Company, Devils Backbone Brewing Company, Random Row Brewing Company, Blue Mountain Brewery, Starr Hill, and Three Notch'd Brewing Company. Sign up for a public or private tour with Cville Hop on Tours, and your transportation is secure.

knowgoodbeer.com

cvillehopontours.com

TASTE LOCALLY PRODUCED SPIRITS
AT VITAE SPIRITS DISTILLERY

Vitae Spirits has two tasting rooms in Charlottesville, its original location at 715 Henry and another just off the Downtown Mall at 101 East Water Street. A tasting outing as a date or with a small group is a great activity for people over 21 years old. A craft distillery, Vitae uses a copper pot still to make its products on-site at its Henry Street location. With a strong interest in using natural ingredients and botanicals to produce its gin, rums, and liqueurs, Vitae may be the only distillery founded and run by a former professor of microbiology.

Sometimes there's education with your gin tasting. On one evening outing to Vitae, we happened upon a presentation being delivered by the University of Virginia's Department of Astronomy on black holes. It was fascinating and an unexpected enhancement to our date-night excursion.

Virginia's laws about tasting rooms are very specific. Guidelines allow for three-ounce tastings per person, per day. In tasting rooms such as Vitae's, guests can try the spirits straight in half-ounce pours, as in tasting flights, or with one-and-a-half ounces of spirits with a mixer in a cocktail.

Try the coffee liqueur—it's amazing!—and explore other local flavors, like the damson gin liqueur or the paw paw liqueur. No one else is making anything like what Vitae has to offer.

Vitae Spirits Distillery Downtown
101 E Water St., 434-260-0920

Vitae Spirits Distillery
715 Henry Ave., 434-270-0317

vitaespirits.com

TOUR THE VINEYARDS
OF CENTRAL VIRGINIA

Thomas Jefferson liked wine, and so does Charlottesville. Following the Monticello Wine Trail is a highly recommended activity any time of year, as a date or with a group; it's not Napa, but it sure is fantastic. At last count, there were more than 30 local wine makers, vineyards, and tasting rooms. Pace yourself; you don't need to visit all 30 in a single afternoon, but we recommend making a plan to get to each over time. Some are large, fancy venues, often the stage for elaborate weddings. Pippin Hill, King Family, Veritas, and Hazy Mountain fit this description and are great for larger group visits. More intimate venues, excellent for romantic dates and proposals, include Wisdom Oak, Cardinal Point, and Flying Fox.

Blue Ridge Wine Excursions provides a smart, comfortable way to experience the wine trail with no worries, suitable for small to large groups.

Each vineyard is as unique as the varietals it offers. Taste, buy, linger, and come back, again and again, to your favorite spots.

Monticello Wine Trail
monticellowinetrail.com

Blue Ridge Wine Excursions
434-242-9313
blueridgewineexcursions.com

TRY A NEW BREW
AT NORTH AMERICAN SAKE BREWERY

Charlottesville likes beer and wine. Hard cider has carved out a niche, and hard seltzers are an up-and-coming locally produced beverage.

A new take on an age-old beverage comes from North American Sake Brewery, a cornerstone in the IX Art Park. Visit to try fresh takes on the naturally gluten-free beverage brewed on-site. Sake is a traditional Japanese beverage made by fermenting rice. North American Sake infuses its menu with different flavors, all served cold.

There are no bars in Virginia; Alcohol Beverage Control law says that there are only restaurants that serve alcohol and that at least 51 percent of sales must be from food. That's good news if you're hungry, because North American Sake offers a delicious menu of items that pair particularly well with sake, giving the restaurant (and tasting room) a unique menu to enjoy during your visit.

522 2nd St. SE, 434-767-8105
pourmeone.com

SIP CIDER IN A DESANCTIFIED CHAPEL
AT POTTER'S CRAFT CIDER

This beautifully restored Episcopal chapel and mission is an idyllic place to drink a variety of hard ciders while listening to music with friends. The stone structure with updated windows and refinished floors gives a rustic vibe and is acoustically sound, a treat for the visiting musicians appearing on a regular schedule. When the weather's good, the grounds are where guests grab tables, and a stage is available for outdoor concerts.

The family-friendly atmosphere also draws cider lovers of all kinds, from the goth and Renaissance Fair crowd to the Vineyard Vines types, from athletes to beer drinkers. They come with dogs and kids to spend the afternoon under the trees or inside the chapel, tasting ciders made of local apples in a variety of styles and flavors.

Try a tasting flight, or buy bottles and cans to take home.

1350 Arrowhead Valley Rd., 434-244-2767
potterscraftcider.com

FIND OUT WHY
BODO'S IS WHERE C'VILLE BUYS BAGELS

Outsiders call it blasphemy. C'villians call it the truth. Bodo's Bagels are the best, anywhere. Don't believe us? Then you haven't been there. A few key tips: know your order before you get to the counter. Bodo's is known for its efficiency and appreciates when customers assist in this effort. Also, never, ever ask for your bagel to be toasted. Bodo's doesn't do that (see efficiency, above). Local tradition has it that it's a high honor to be the day's first customer with the coveted "#001" printed receipt. Can you get up that early?

1418 Emmet St., 434-977-9598
505 Preston Ave. (Downtown), 434-293-5224
1609 University Ave. (on the Corner), 434-293-6021

bodosbagels.com

TRY A SLICE
IN A COLLEGE TOWN

What's a college town without awesome pizza? I don't ever want to find out. The Charlottesville area has several particularly popular lauded pizza joints: Lampo Neapolitan Pizzeria, Mellow Mushroom, Crozet Pizza (and its near-Grounds cousin, Crozet Pizza at Buddhist Biker Bar), Dr. Ho's Humble Pie, Christian's Pizza, Vita Nova, and Anna's Pizza No. 5. Each is unique in crust preparation, sauce flavor and allotment, topping selections, and overall ambiance. All offer takeout. Christian's, Vita Nova, and Benny DeLuca's are by-the-slice joints. The only thing to do is try each kind and choose your favorite.

Places to Try a Slice

Lampo
205 Monticello Rd., 434-244-3226

Mellow Mushroom
1321 W Main St., 434-972-9366

Crozet Pizza
5794 Three Notch'd Rd., Crozet, 434-823-2132
crozetpizza.com

Dr. Ho's Humble Pie
4916 Plank Rd., North Garden, 434-245-0000
doctorhoshumblepie.com

Christian's Pizza
118 W Main St., 434-977-9688

Vita Nova
310 E. Main St., 434-977-0162

Anna's Pizza No. 5
115 Maury Ave., 434-977-6228

TRY A PALETA
AT LA FLOR MICHOACANA

In parts of Mexico, *la michoacana* is what locals call the corner ice cream shop. There are more than 30,000 businesses in Mexico that use *la michoacana* in their name.

In Charlottesville, the place to go for ice cream and authentic Mexican paletas is La Flor Michoacana. Find this charming and popular paleteria on Cherry Avenue, and be prepared to be overwhelmed by choice. Is it possible to choose from so many flavors and options?

Go for the ice cream, but be prepared to change your mind and choose from a gorgeous array of colorful, fruit-filled paletas, fancy Mexican popsicles made with fresh fruit and cream. Try yellow cherry, tres leches, guava, mango, or black cherry cheesecake.

La Flor is also the spot to buy a piñata and a variety of candies imported from Mexico to delight guests at your next party.

We can never choose just one paleta or ice cream flavor, so it's not uncommon for us to get some to go to keep in our freezer (though possibly only until after dinner).

601 Cherry Ave., 434-984-1603
laflormichoacana.com

GREASE YOUR SPOON
AT THE WHITE SPOT

I wouldn't recommend making a visit to the White Spot a daily occurrence. Any diet would suffer from overindulgence in this historic burger joint's specialties, but once in a while—or even once in a lifetime—the Gus Burger is a must. A departure from the hifalutin gourmet offerings of restaurants downtown or in Belmont, the White Spot steps back in time to an era free from cholesterol concerns.

For some, the greasy spoon treatment is the perfect way to cure what ails ya. Many a Gus Burger has been consumed as a late-night or early-morning meal, following what is often a Corner pub crawl. The Gus Burger, as fans know, is an all-beef patty topped with cheese and a fried egg. Add enhancements and fries as you see fit. If you're willing to take it up a notch, try the Motor Burger, which is a double cheeseburger, a fried egg, and a thick slab of country ham.

A trip to the White Spot is inexpensive and worth the walk (there's rarely a place to park, but you'll need a walk before and after anyway), so plan to visit the Grounds, thoroughly explore the Corner, and treat yourself to some good, greasy eats.

1407 University Ave.
434-295-9899

MEET FOR COFFEE
AT A LOCAL SHOP

Charlottesvillians are fairly serious about their caffeine delivery mechanisms. Are the beans roasted in-house? Where did the coffee come from? Is it fair trade? What notes and aromas will I detect in the brewing? Is it French press, single cup pour-over, or vacuum brewed? Our local coffeehouses are some of our shining stars. Try Mudhouse, Shenandoah Joe, and Milli Coffee Roasters for starters. Take a tour and taste-test your favorites. Coffee is often an excuse for our community members to gather, and all are great places to work, drink multiple cups, and meet friends or colleagues.

Mudhouse Downtown
213 W Main St., 434-984-6833
mudhouse.com

Shenandoah Joe
945 Preston Ave., 434-295-4563
shenandoahjoe.com

Milli Coffee Roasters
400 Preston Ave., #150, 434-906-0250
millicoffeeroasters.com

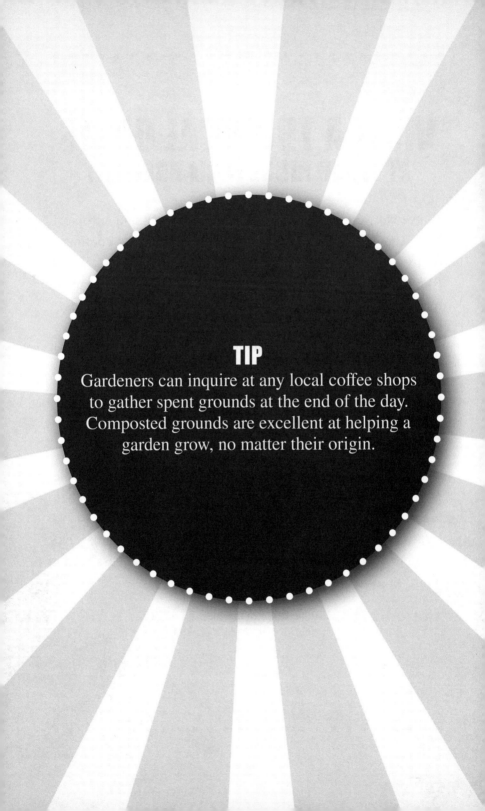

TIP

Gardeners can inquire at any local coffee shops to gather spent grounds at the end of the day. Composted grounds are excellent at helping a garden grow, no matter their origin.

VISIT A TROPICAL OASIS
AT WOOD RIDGE FARM BREWERY

Where can you find palm trees, sand volleyball, and a tropical bar? About 30 minutes from town, a magical oasis continues to grow, with frog ponds and banana trees. It's called Wood Ridge Farm Brewery. On our first visit, we were enchanted by the large, two-story, rough-hewn saloon serving house-brewed beer. The enterprise, a vision of its owner, Barry Wood, continues to expand, with food truck service providing bar snacks like totchos and mozzarella sticks, bocce ball, fire pits, and a wood-fired pizza oven. Cornhole is taken seriously at Wood Ridge, and tournament night is Thursday. The new tropical bar area is ready for evenings of live music, suitable for Jimmy Buffett covers.

The views are spectacular. Peacocks and hens stroll the grounds while you sip your beer and sway to the tunes. When night falls, the farm lights up with hundreds of fairy and bistro lights. We recommend trying all the different seating areas, but the upper deck of the saloon in a pair of rocking chairs with a house-brewed ale is hard to beat.

165 Old Ridge Rd., Lovingston, 434-422-6225
woodridgefarmbreweryva.com

SATISFY YOUR APPETITE
AT DAIRY MARKET

The words "high-end" and "food court" don't typically show up together, but that is exactly how we described Dairy Market after our first visit. The self-described food hall is a collection of diverse restaurants with common seating areas, bookended by two different enclosed restaurants. On one end, there's Starr Hill Brewery. On the other is a white tablecloth restaurant called South and Central with a menu shaped by the flavors of South and Central America. In the middle, guests find a wide variety of eats, including wood-fired pizzas, fried fish, Filipino street food, burgers, Thai food, and deli sandwiches. It's a great lunch or dinner stop for a group or a family with various tastes!

Milkman's Bar, at the back and center of the food hall experience, prides itself on stunningly beautiful craft cocktails and an array of nonalcoholic drinks for the non-imbibers in your crew. For dessert, stop by the real dairy experience of Moo Thru, a Culpeper original favorite, for a cup or a cone of your favorite ice cream.

946 Grady Ave., 434-326-4552
dairymarketcville.com

SIP YOUR TEA
AT TWISTED BRANCH TEA BAZAAR

If the coffee shop scene is not for you, the Twisted Branch Tea Bazaar might be. Tea connoisseurs and tobacco fans flock upstairs to the Downtown Mall's only tea bazaar and hookah bar for a caffeine rush and tobacco hit. It might seem odd or dated, but the atmosphere is 1960s chic, and the crowd is there to study, work, visit with one another, or just ponder life. Seating is lush with cushions and pillows, small-group rooms, and a cozy outdoor patio. Don't harsh the mellow. Teas and hookahs of many flavors abound. This spot also plays host to musicians on occasion and offers vegetarian and vegan food items.

414 E Main St., 434-293-9947
teabazaar.com

TIP
Check the schedule for live music events in the evenings, and come back to the Tea Bazaar for a different kind of experience.

ORDER A SLICE OF NOSTALGIA
AT TIMBERLAKE'S

There are two drugstores on the Downtown Mall. One is a national chain. The other is a locally owned vehicle for time travel. Timberlake's Drug Store delivers prescriptions free of charge within city limits. You can still find the soap your grandmother used or the shaving cream your grandfather favored on its shelves. Once you've spent time browsing the glass cases and stocked shelves and admiring the vintage posters from the 1960s on the walls, you suddenly realize there's more to Timberlake's.

Beyond the retail front of the operation, there's an old-timey lunch counter, its menu the same, one imagines, as it's been for the past hundred years. That, of course, is what makes it so good—the BLTs, the egg salad sandwiches, and the slices of pie served à la mode if you'd like. But don't forget to save room for a milkshake.

It's part nostalgic trip, part museum piece, so don't forget to browse the photographs of regulars that line the walls. They're not relics of the past—they're photos of the people who might be enjoying a Timberlake's lunch right that very moment.

Plop yourself down on a red vinyl stool at the counter, order up something you haven't had in a long time, and enjoy the memories that come flooding in along with a surprising amount of sunlight.

322 E Main St., 434-295-9155

TIP

Order one of the men on the menu—sandwiches, that is, all with masculine names like Mr. George (ham salad), Mr. Darden (egg salad with bacon), or Mr. Coleman (pastrami and swiss on rye).

MUSIC
AND ENTERTAINMENT

CATCH A SUNSET
AT SENTARA MARTHA JEFFERSON HOSPITAL

Pantops Mountain is a populated section of the city, teaming with businesses, car dealerships, and homes. It's an excellent vantage point for catching gorgeous sunsets—something about the altitude and atmosphere, as many locals will attest. The outdoor amphitheater at Sentara Martha Jefferson Hospital is a special venue, ideal for watching day turn to night. The hospital takes advantage of its lovely grounds and welcoming venue by hosting Sunsets with Sentara, inviting the public and providing free live music from 5:30 to 8:30 p.m. on select summer evenings. Make sure to bring a phone or a camera to catch those bright pink skies, but leave your pets at home.

500 Martha Jefferson Dr., 434-654-7000

ENJOY LOCAL THEATER
AT LIVE ARTS

Live Arts is just the ticket to scratch your theatrical itch. Participate in or join the audience for Charlottesville's all-volunteer community theater, established in 1990. The great thing about community theater is just that; it's a true community collaboration. Live Arts brings together all-volunteer casts, producers, set builders, choreographers, and directors for some surprisingly well-done productions. Looking for a bargain? Try a "Pay What You Can" Wednesday evening performance, keeping in mind your donation helps keep the theater alive.

In addition to year-round theater productions, Live Arts offers programs and workshops to teach the arts to both adults and children.

123 E Water St., 434-977-4177
livearts.org

FIND YOUR VENUE
FOR LIVE MUSIC

See a concert at one of several venues: the Jefferson, the Paramount, John Paul Jones Arena, or the Ting Pavilion. Each spot has its own unique vibe. The Jefferson is a smaller, more intimate space, and the Paramount is a fancier, more formal historic theater. John Paul Jones Arena is where the University of Virginia holds its home basketball games, so expect big names like Dave Matthews (who got his start in a bar called Miller's on the Downtown Mall). The Pavilion—the white mushroom-shaped structure on the far east end of the Downtown Mall—is an outdoor entertainment venue from late spring through early fall. Each Friday in the summer, bands perform as part of the free series Fridays After Five.

Charlottesville is home to Red Light Management, the artist management company founded by Coran Capshaw, manager of the Dave Matthews Band. By virtue of its long relationships in the music industry, Charlottesville has the ability to attract much bigger and better acts and a wider variety of musical and theatrical entertainment to the area than do most towns its size. It's not often that you find a place like Charlottesville on the tour list for the kinds of bands these venues attract, but C'ville is a frequent stop for sold-out shows.

Venues for Live Music

The Jefferson Theater
110 E Main St., 434-245-4980
jeffersontheater.com

The Paramount Theater
215 E Main St., 434-979-1333
theparamount.net

John Paul Jones Arena
295 Massie Rd., 434-243-4960
johnpauljonesarena.com

Ting Pavilion
700 E Main St., 434-245-4910
tingpavilion.com

WITNESS A SPECTACLE
AT CLAW

CLAW, otherwise known as Charlottesville Lady Arm Wrestlers, is wildly celebrated in our little town. We love our lady arm wrestlers! Their names are as entertaining as the event (and the costumes). See the Homewrecker, Malice in Wonderland, Stiletto Southpaw, and Tropical Depression at their best! CLAW is a bunch of beefed-up local gals with amazing guns competing for bragging rights and upper-body-strength mojo, all while raising money for charitable organizations in town. Part carnival sideshow, part theatrical spectacle, and, I suppose, part sporting event, our town's baddest ladies dress up and throw down for charity under the tent at Champion Brewing Company.

324 6th St. SE, 434-295-2739
clawville.org

TIP
Champion Brewing Company, the host for CLAW events, is a locally owned craft brewery with award-winning brews. Try its Shower Beer (a pilsner) or Missile IPA, or branch out and try its latest brew on tap.

EMBARK ON A STAYCATION
IN CHARLOTTESVILLE

Stay at a boutique inn or bed and breakfast. Better yet, stay at home—someone else's, that is. Stay Charlottesville enables you to "live like a local," making it possible to rent space in some pretty spectacular homes. Renovating? Escaping the in-laws? Check out one of these places. Or, if you are from somewhere else, there's nothing better than a short- or long-term stay in a finely appointed, perfectly situated property that is truly home (someone else's home, but for a time—and a price—yours). There are dozens of charming spots, both in town and in the country. Stay in one for a visit, or, if you live in Charlottesville, find an excuse to spend a night away from home.

434-977-0442
staycharlottesville.com

TIP
The variety of vacation homes available through Stay Charlottesville includes properties large enough to host an entire wedding or family reunion.

CRASH A CONCERT
BY EAVESDROPPING FROM
THE BELMONT BRIDGE

Concert tickets are costly. Prudent concert-goers need to pick and choose which acts to see. If you're on the fence, here's an alternative. Stand on the sidewalk just to the north of the Belmont Bridge on Avon Street, behind the Ting Pavilion on the far east end of the Downtown Mall, and enjoy a concert. Commune with the other freeloaders during this unique experience of enjoying the backstage pass of a concert for free.

Big acts pack the sidewalk, so determine your crowd comfort level before you go, and plan to move along if authorities request it.

TIP

Outdoor dining on the Downtown Mall or on Market Street can also provide enough proximity to overhear a concert, without the hassle of the crowds.

HANG OUT
AT MILLER'S

If you're a Dave Matthews Band fan, then you probably know that the legendary local singer got his start working and playing at Miller's, a classic bar on the Downtown Mall. Miller's has great bar food, but the ambiance is strictly saloon. The hangout, more than 30 years old, boasts a third-floor pool room and a full kitchen open until midnight. Miller's also offers ample seating in its outdoor patio section—prime real estate on Charlottesville's Downtown Mall. Go for live music, beer, and well drinks. And as a DMB fan, revel in the historic significance of Charlottesville's favorite musical son.

109 W Main St., 434-971-8511
millersdowntown.com

TIP
Take a stroll off the Downtown Mall across Water Street to see the Pink Warehouse, once home to Dave Matthews.

GO BACK TO HIGH SCHOOL,
JUST FOR A NIGHT

It's OK—it's only temporary. The award-winning orchestra at Charlottesville High School is worth a listen. Nationally recognized for excellence, the orchestra has 150 members and is composed of a string ensemble and a concert orchestra. Supported in part by the generosity of the Dave Matthews Band Fund, administered by the Charlottesville Community Area Foundation. The orchestra has the orchestra has taken top prizes at music festivals in London, New York, Boston, Atlanta, and Chicago, to name just a few.

Not to be overshadowed by the city's high school, Albemarle High School has an equally recognized drama department. The spring musical at AHS is a widely attended production, with much more than parents and fellow students filling the auditorium for every sold-out performance; it's a real community-wide event. Two consecutive years have had the community at large voting the AHS musical as the favorite local play—of all the theaters and all the plays in town—in a weekly publication's annual poll.

TRY BOARD GAMES
WITH LOCAL CONNECTIONS

You may have heard of the board game Settlers of Catan, but you probably weren't aware that the business of the game is managed in Charlottesville by Catan Studio. With more than 27 million games sold and worldwide competitions held in Germany each year, it comes as a surprise to enthusiasts that the brand is run right here in central Virginia. Players of the game take the role of settlers, acquiring resources, trading, and building civilizations to earn points and win.

A new, lesser-known board game from another company with local roots is Chickapig. With Kickstarter funding and support from its owner's friend Dave Matthews, Chickapig is sweeping the nation. It's fun, silly, and strategic, involving chicken-pig hybrids, cows, and lots of cow poop. Kardinal Hall, a downtown beer garden and restaurant, has Chickapig Tuesdays where anyone can come to learn and play.

catan.com

chickapig.com

Kardinal Hall
722 Preston Ave., 434-295-4255
kardinalhall.com

IMMERSE YOURSELF IN ART
AT IX ART PARK

The Looking Glass at IX Art Park is Charlottesville's only immersive art experience. More than a dozen local artists collaborated to create a living museum for guests to wander, wonder, and enjoy. The exhibit includes an enchanted forest packed with sound, light, and color. The Looking Glass includes digital and tactile art. Visitors are invited to touch the art; doing so sometimes elicits unexpected responses!

All ages are encouraged to attend, but children under the age of 13 must be accompanied by an adult. If you're sensory-sensitive, this may not be the exhibit for you, but the Looking Glass offers a free downloadable coloring book on its website for young children and those who would rather experience and enjoy the art at home.

Before its development in 2014, the space was the former site of the Frank Ix and Sons textile factory. The concrete-and-steel warehouse and its surroundings were all but abandoned at that time. Owner Ludwig Kuttner had a vision to turn the space into a vibrant, engaging, inviting property and worked with a team of like-minded people to create the ever-evolving project.

522 2nd St. SE
ixartpark.org/lookingglass

● ●

GO FULL TILT
AT DECADES ARCADE

Ophthalmologist and entrepreneur Dr. Paul Yates collects vintage pinball machines—no matter their condition. Yates takes the time to restore art, repair broken machines, and replace missing parts.

In 2018 Yates opened Paul's Pinball Palace, giving the public access to his museum of games. Interest in the pinball emporium was enthusiastic. With an all-you-can-play $10 fee, it was a great form of evening entertainment. As the business (and Yates) continued to collect machines, from pinball machines and video games to larger formats including air hockey and Dance Dance Revolution, the arcade grew and grew. A small but dedicated group of fellow gamers donated machines and their expertise for upkeep of the collection. Larger space later opened in a warehouse in Belmont, and in the fall of 2018 Paul's Pinball Palace became Decades Arcade, so named because the games in the collection span the decades from the '50s to the present.

Decades hosts a local pinball league, has a dedicated game repair day, and holds private events during the workweek. Public hours are held on the weekends. The fee remains a low $12 per gamer for an entire day of play time.

221 Carlton Rd., 434-962-7986
decadesarcade.com

SPY SWEET SUNSETS
FROM CARTER MOUNTAIN

If you have been in Charlottesville in the fall, you may have found your way to Carter Mountain Orchard for apple picking. It is adjacent to Thomas Jefferson's Monticello, so half a million visitors to the former president's residence pass the sign for apple picking each fall. It's a popular spot!

Carter Mountain has wisely expanded its draw from parents, kids, and school groups to crowds of grownups for outdoor evening events. Sunset views, hard cider, food trucks, and live music that are part of summertime events make the mountaintop the place to be. On extra-hot days, enjoy a cider or wine slushie.

There's no better place in town to watch the sun set—or a storm roll in—than the top of Carter Mountain. Wind Down Wednesday events are more chill events, with acoustic sets and grab-and-go food. Thursday evening's Sunset Series events are a party, with food trucks and musical acts that run the gamut. Check the website for the full lineup and to secure tickets for any evening event.

For daytime visits, don't miss the country store and bakery, known for the apple cider donuts, apple butter, and apple pies. Buy some to eat before you make it back down the mountain and some to have later at home.

1435 Carters Mountain Trl., 434-977-1833
chilesfamilyorchards.com/carter-mountain-orchard

VIEW GREAT FLICKS
AT THE VIRGINIA FILM FESTIVAL

Each year in early November, Charlottesville plays host to Hollywood. A long weekend is packed with more than 100 films, including independent films, fascinating documentaries, feature debuts, and classics, along with visits from Virginia filmmakers and exciting special guests. Famous producers, actors, and directors make appearances at the Virginia Film Festival, speaking at screenings of their films and making themselves available for audience interaction. The annual lineup announcement is eagerly anticipated, and guests buy their tickets well in advance to ensure good seats.

Are you a college student? Free tickets are available for those currently enrolled at the University of Virginia.

virginiafilmfestival.org

CATCH A SHOW
AT THE PARAMOUNT

The historic Paramount Theater should be on your list of places to visit. It's a beautifully restored theater in the middle of the Charlottesville Downtown Mall marked by its vertical blade signage, a frequently photographed landmark. The venue is used for concerts, ballets, operas, speakers, nonprofit galas, and more. An event at the Paramount always feels very special. Visit around the holidays for a special movie night featuring a classic like *It's a Wonderful Life* or *White Christmas*. Take the afternoon for holiday shopping before this annual family movie tradition. When you emerge from the theater into the dark amid the marquee lights and the crisp cold of December (and, if you're lucky, a few picturesque snowflakes falling), there's no chance you'll be able to escape the holiday spirit.

215 E Main St., 434-979-1333
theparamount.net

TAKE OFF EARLY
FOR A FREE CONCERT AT THE PAVILION

From mid-April to mid-September, enjoy weekly free concerts in a very family-friendly atmosphere. Fridays After Five is this town's favorite live concert series. The audience is populated with people just getting off work, as well as whole families enjoying a night out in the summertime weather. Concessions and food trucks are available for al fresco dinner options. The lawn at the Ting Pavilion is a favorite hangout for dancing toddlers and their moms. It's a great way to greet neighbors and friends, hear some often local music, and start off the weekend with a community celebration.

Fundraising opportunities are available to nonprofits who agree to staff beer trucks for Fridays After Five, so order your brew knowing it goes, in part, to support a local charity.

700 E Main St., 434-245-4910
tingpavilion.com

GAZE AT THE STARS
AT VERITAS WINERY

Wine and starry nights are a perfect pairing. Veritas Winery takes it a step further and adds live music to the mix. A popular summertime event, Starry Nights at Veritas invites guests to bring lawn chairs and blankets and sit out under the great big expanse of sky while enjoying live music and wonderful Veritas wines. In the off season, there's no better winery living room than Veritas Winery, where you can get cozy on leather couches under soaring ceilings before an enormous stone fireplace. It's the very best place to wait out some inclement weather with a glass of wine.

151 Veritas Ln., Afton, 540-456-8000
veritaswines.com/events

GO WITH YOUR GROUP
TO THE MOVIES

Until 2012, Charlottesville seemed like the last small town in America without a state-of-the-art multiplex with an IMAX theater and stadium seating. In short order, the area gained three with separate personalities: Stonefield, Violet Crown, and Alamo Drafthouse. Stonefield is a huge, mainstream, blockbuster-hosting movie theater. Violet Crown, our Downtown Mall theater, offers reserved seating and small-theater experiences with beer, wine, and food available to take in with you. Alamo Drafthouse also has reserved seating, and waiters will serve you food and drinks right at your seat! Now we feel even better than the rest of America plunking down $100-200 for a family of four to see the latest action-adventure film.

Regal Stonefield ScreenX and IMAX
1954 Swanson Dr., 844-462-7342
shopsatstonefield.com

Violet Crown Charlottesville
200 W Main St., 434-529-3000
charlottesville.violetcrown.com

Alamo Drafthouse Cinema
375 Merchant Walk Sq., 434-326-5056
drafthouse.com/Charlottesville

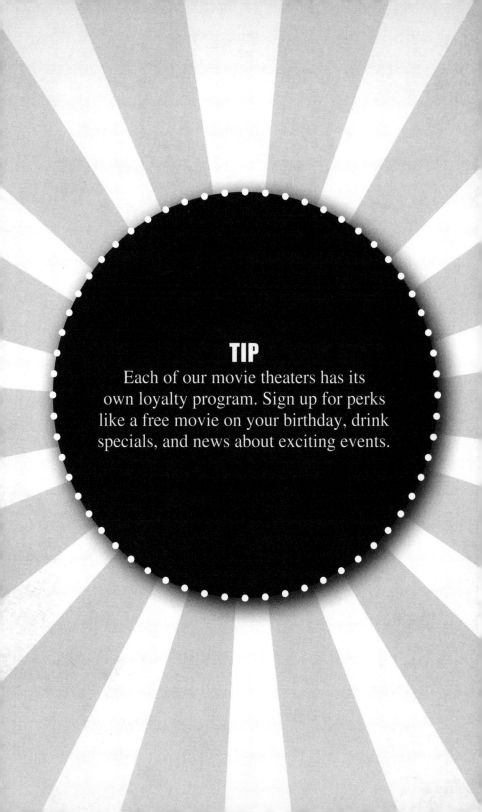

TIP

Each of our movie theaters has its own loyalty program. Sign up for perks like a free movie on your birthday, drink specials, and news about exciting events.

EXPERIENCE AUTHENTIC SHAKESPEARE
AT BLACKFRIARS PLAYHOUSE

Down the road, over the mountain, and into the valley, Staunton, Virginia, is home to the American Shakespeare Center and the Blackfriars Playhouse. Known as the American home of Shakespeare, this excellent theater is the world's only full re-creation of Shakespeare's indoor theater. The actors perform in historically accurate theater space with no elaborate sets, microphones, or speakers and with the actors sharing the same lighting as the audience. It's a unique experience of Elizabethan work, just a short drive from downtown Charlottesville.

The Blackfriars Playhouse also puts on an annual production of *A Christmas Carol*, a sold-out family favorite.

10 S Market St., Staunton, 540-851-1733
americanshakespearecenter.com

TIP
Make time to walk around downtown Staunton, where you'll find charming shops, excellent restaurants, and beautiful homes.

SEE A TINY CONCERT
IN THE GARAGE

In what must be the tiniest concert venue, a brick one-car garage faces a hill in a park in Downtown Charlottesville. During the day, it doesn't look like much, but on a concert night, the Garage transforms. Fans plop down on the grass in Market Street Park and face the open garage, where bands set up shop and entertain everyone within earshot. The Garage is on First Street between Market and Jefferson streets, next to Hill & Wood Funeral Service. Aside from concerts, the Garage sometimes hosts art openings or potluck dinners. A Kickstarter success story, the venue was able to raise more than $10,000 to repair a hole in a brick wall and make needed improvements to the interior in 2013. Clearly, this is a spot well-loved by the C'ville community.

100 W Jefferson St.
thegaragecville.com

TIP

Bring ground cover and sit on the hill in the park opposite the Garage for stellar VIP seating.

SPORTS
AND RECREATION

TAKE A WALK IN THE DARK
ON THE BLUE RIDGE TUNNEL TRAIL

If you like exploring in the dark, have we got the experience for you! The Blue Ridge Tunnel Trail is the best dark-as-midnight daytime adventure. You absolutely must have a flashlight, headlamp, bike light, or other trusty illumination. The tunnel is nearly a mile long, making it impossible to see end-to-end. Bright lights will enable you to see the plant life and creatures that enjoy the damp underground life. Keep an eye out for frogs and salamanders!

There are two official parking areas to reach the tunnel. They fill up fast, so plan your hike (or bike) through the tunnel early in the day. The eastern end is at the Afton Depot off of Route 6, and it's a 15-minute hike to reach the eastern tunnel entrance. This is the more polished tunnel entrance, with quicker access from the parking area.

The western tunnel access is off Route 250 West toward Waynesboro from the interstate turnoff. The hike from the parking area is rather long and hilly, so if you're traveling with young kids or folks with physical challenges, you may wish to choose the eastern access instead. Hike or bike through and back to return to your parking area of choice.

West Trailhead
483 Three Notched Mountain Hwy., Waynesboro

East Trailhead
215 Afton Depot Ln., Afton

Photo courtesy of Hunter Chorey

HIKE AN URBAN LOOP
ON THE RIVANNA TRAIL

You might catch a glimpse here and there of a dark green, diamond-shaped insignia on the side of the road, across from a parking lot, or behind a baseball diamond. Let your feet follow your curiosity to the Rivanna Trail, an urban trail that loops around and through city sights.

The Rivanna Trail is an urban wilderness hiking trail built and maintained by volunteers. The 20-mile trail includes sections that range from easy to strenuous, meandering by—and sometimes over—creeks, streams, and rivers. The trail is only continuous if you're willing to do a few slight off-trail jogs over city roads, through waterways (sometimes with stepping stones), or through some soggy, muddy spots. Some of our favorite hikes include out-and-back sections of the trail, rather than trying to do the whole loop in a day.

Along the way, you'll experience gentle streams, steep climbs, sweet bridges across waterways, open meadows, backyard views, parks and ballfields, highway glimpses, graffitied underpasses, and much more.

The Rivanna Trail is a community treasure for exercise, relaxation, and nature-related education. With several access points, the trail connects many neighborhoods and six city parks. It is open for hiking and jogging from sunup to sundown. Because most of the trail passes over private property, hikers are asked to stay on the trail and to keep dogs on leashes at all times. Trail guides are available at visitors' centers, at local outdoor and running stores, and on the Rivanna Trail website.

Once a month, the Rivanna Trail Foundation hosts a work party, which is a gathering of volunteers to tackle the creation of bridges and paths, to create new sections of trail, and to clear and make safer the existing paths.

rivannatrails.org

● ●

GO UP IN THE AIR
IN A HOT AIR BALLOON

Conditions must be right for this high-altitude treat, and it's not recommended for anyone who isn't reasonably fit or who is afraid of heights. On a low-wind day, if those obstacles are settled, the vista of the Blue Ridge Mountains, the lush green of Southern horse farms, and sleepy rivers cannot be beat. A gently rising and coasting hot air balloon is the only way to gain the slow-moving, high-level perspective of the area.

Some hot air balloon launches take place from the grounds of the Boar's Head in Ivy. On still days, keep an eye on the sky and you might catch a colorful glimpse of the balloons.

Blue Ridge Ballooning
434-589-6213
blueridgeballoon.com

Monticello Country Ballooning
434-996-9008
virginiahotairballoon.com

WATCH POLO
AT KING FAMILY VINEYARDS

Before I lived in Virginia, I'd never seen a polo game—televised or live. Polo is a sport often showcased by a well-heeled kind of community that only East Coast towns seem to boast. It is, in part, an excuse for women to don a sundress and an otherwise-ridiculous-if-worn-anywhere-else hat. Wear shoes suitable for divot stomping—the halftime practice of tamping down the torn-up turf. It's a popular tradition, and people of all ages will take to the field to stomp around. Make sure you're paying attention when the athletes and the horses want to get back on the field, or the lawn may not be the only thing that gets stomped! Polo matches are free and open to the public. Wine is *not* free, but tastings and a shared bottle or two are recommended. Try the Viognier, made from the state grape of Virginia. There's nothing that will make you feel more like a part of the upper echelon than sipping a glass of Viognier while observing a polo match (with rules you barely understand) in the shadow of the Blue Ridge Mountains.

6550 Roseland Farm, Crozet, 434-823-7800
kingfamilyvineyards.com

FLOAT, KAYAK, OR CANOE
ON A RIVER

A summer without spending time on one of Central Virginia's peaceful rivers simply isn't a summer at all. The Rivanna, James, and Shenandoah rivers all have easy access nearby, and several rental companies can hook you up with the necessary equipment if you don't own your own. A day trip of four hours or so leaves plenty of time to play in the water and picnic on the beach. Make sure you have lifejackets—rivers are monitored by local police, and not having a flotation device may earn you a hefty fine. It's also important to pay attention to river levels. A lot of rain may make the river levels too high and unsafe; a drought can make them too low and not much fun.

Lack confidence in your river-paddling skills? Sign up for an introduction to kayaking class or a paddleboard core workout through Rivanna River Company.

Rivanna River Company
434-218-2052
rivannarivercompany.com

RIDE YOUR BIKE
THROUGH THE SCENIC COUNTRYSIDE

Bicyclists enjoy many excellent scenic routes in and around Charlottesville. The route from Edge Valley Road to Plank Road is a favorite. This ride is more than 2.7 miles of valley, first settled in the 18th century. Edge Valley Road runs from Taylor's Gap Road at its eastern end to historic Plank Road to the west. The ride begins with views of a stunning century-old Georgian manor home and the remains of an ancient cabin. Follow along the Middle Branch North Fork Hardware River in picture-perfect countryside, passing marshy wetlands and an artist's vision of an old red barn in the middle of a rolling hay field. Roll into Batesville, an unincorporated community in Albemarle County founded in 1760. In pre–Civil War days, the town was a station on the direct path for agricultural goods to get to Eastern customers. At Batesville, you can go left to Pippin Hill Farm and Vineyards for a visit to the tasting room, then on to Dr. Ho's Humble Pie to finish the day off right.

cvillebikeclub.org

TAKE YOUR DOG
FOR A ROMP

Charlottesville is definitely a town for dog lovers, with a well-supported no-kill animal shelter and many pet-friendly venues. But nothing delights a dog more than a romp in a dog park with fellow furry friends. Dog parks are located at Darden Towe Park, Azalea Park, and Chris Greene Lake Park.

On a relatively dry weekend afternoon, pack up the dog—or borrow one or two (but not three . . . there are rules about these things) if you don't have your own—and head out to the Chris Greene Lake dog park, the only park with lake access for dog swimming escapades. It's hard to be grumpy in the presence of bounding, fetching, and joyous animals. The first time I stumbled upon the dog park on a hike, I was sans canine but still visited to watch all the pups playing and swimming. Dog people are generally friendly, and there's a ready-made topic of conversation as your animals sniff each other and romp about.

Darden Towe Park
1445 Darden Towe Park

Azalea Park Dog Park
304 Old Lynchburg Rd.

Chris Green Lake Park
4748 Chris Greene Lake Rd.

WALK THE GROUNDS
AND STREAK ... THE LAWN

College campuses are often beautiful, and the Grounds at the University of Virginia are no exception. The Grounds of UVA (don't call it campus!) feature beautiful historic buildings, manicured lawns, picturesque trees, elegant gardens, and a fantastic serpentine wall. Make sure you take a guided tour with at least an alumnus if not a current student. Don't miss Edgar Allan Poe's room; the Lawn, its pavilions, and their surrounding rooms of upper-echelon students; the Amphitheatre; and the Rotunda.

Of course, we can't recommend that anyone disrobe and run across the Lawn, the pristine yard in front of the Rotunda, but some say the tradition at the University of Virginia includes just that—streaking during the first snowfall of winter, specifically. Use your own good judgment, or just recognize that the tradition exists and strategically time a walk on the Grounds to see if you can spot a traditionalist.

virginia.edu

TAKE A WALK IN THE WOODS
ALONG THE APPALACHIAN TRAIL

Bill Bryson's book *A Walk in the Woods: Rediscovering America on the Appalachian Trail* could inspire just about anyone to lace up those hiking boots and hit the trail. The book documents a pair's journey on the Appalachian Trail (or AT), a trail that stretches from Georgia to Maine. Plenty of miles of the AT run through Virginia, and particularly through the Charlottesville area. If you don't have time to hike the entire AT, get a local taste; perhaps you'll be inspired to try the full trip one day. For the less ambitious, there are other, shorter hikes with big payoffs of vistas, waterfalls, or just plain beautiful scenery. The important thing is to get out on a trail, whether for a little bit or a long time, somewhere in the area. You won't be sorry.

Hikes we like include Humpback Rocks, Old Rag, Spy Rock, Crabtree Falls, Sugar Hollow, Blue Hole, and the Rivanna Trail. Riverview Park, close to downtown, is good if you're short on time and can't get to the country.

appalachiantrail.org

CLIMB A WALL
AT ROCKY TOP

Are you a veteran climber? Or perhaps you are rock-wall-curious. If you've always wondered whether rock climbing is the activity for you, Rocky Top Climbing is the safe indoor venue (including guided instruction) to find out. For more experienced climbers, the centrally located climbing gym offers an indoor venue to help you keep in shape or hone your skills for your next outdoor adventure.

The walls are 13 feet high and provide 4,500 square feet of climbing practice. Expert climbers set new scenarios each week, keeping the problems challenging for visitors. Rocky Top has youth programs, too, for kids who are climbing the walls at home and need a place to learn how to build those skills for the outside world.

1729 Allied St., 434-981-3306
rockytopclimbing.com

SIT ON A TRACTOR SEAT
AT THE TOP OF BEAR DEN MOUNTAIN

Walk the trail at Bear Den Mountain in Shenandoah National Park and end up at the top of the mountain, where a semicircle of tractor seats has been planted in the ground. The family that owned the land put them there (no, we can't grow tractor seats in Virginia soil), and there they've stayed for decades. Have a seat and admire the view of the Blue Ridge Mountains.

Bear Den Trail Center
18393 Blueridge Mountain Rd., Bluemont, 540-554-8708
bearsdencenter.org

TIP

Bear Den is close to the Greenwood Country Store, an excellent stop for picnic provisions before your hike.

PLAY FOR BODY AND MIND
AT WILDROCK

The mental health benefits of being outside in nature are well-known. Childhood development benefits from connecting with nature as well. Wildrock, a three-and-a-half-acre property developed with psychology and mental health in mind, is an outdoor play, discovery, and retreat center. Wildrock has been created by countless volunteers and community partners. From Sally Mander, a one-of-a-kind piece created onsite by an artisan, to a giant nest, created and maintained by several volunteer groups over the years, to the crafted play materials throughout the playscape and Barn Center, visitors have an experience at Wildrock that they truly can't find anywhere else.

Located adjacent to the Patricia Ann Byrom Forest Preserve Park (the largest park in Albemarle County), the playscape features a stream and pastures framed by mountains in the distance. There's a barn and a hobbit house for indoor exploration and a walking labyrinth to traverse.

Make a reservation to take your family—or all the neighborhood kids—and play alongside them, discovering nature right in our backyard.

6600 Blackwells Hollow Rd., Crozet, 434-825-8631
wildrock.org

GET ABOARD
AN AMTRAK TRAIN

Sometimes the best thing to do in Charlottesville is get out of Charlottesville. Amtrak makes taking a train super easy. You can pop up to DC without breaking a sweat. Board the train on a Friday afternoon and get to NYC as the clubs are starting to hop. Great weekends also await in Philadelphia and Boston with this inexpensive, low-stress way to travel. With the station located downtown, university students and visitors can come and go easily, and working commuters can zip around the Northeast, working with onboard Wi-Fi in total comfort.

810 W Main St., 434-296-4559
amtrak.com

NOTE
Charlottesville's Union Station is the third-busiest Amtrak station in Virginia. It is served by the Cardinal, Crescent, and Northeast Regional passenger trains.

TAKE A BIKE TOUR
OF THE C'VILLE MURAL PROJECT

There are more than 40 murals around Charlottesville! It's a challenge to find them all, so make a day of it and conduct a mural scavenger hunt. Most are outdoors and easily seen by the public. Others are indoors, and you have to know where to go to find them.

Enter the Charlottesville Mural Project. The Bridge Progressive Arts Initiative is behind this enterprise, connecting the properties willing to host the artwork and the artists interested in creating it. To make it easy, the initiative has created a map on its website with a suggested two-mile mural walk, a seven-mile bike loop, or a public transportation route to see many of the works of art.

One of the more visible works is *Together We Grow*, a collaborative effort from designer/artist Jake Van Yahres, painter Christy Baker, and students from Charlottesville High School. This mural, which depicts trees as people holding hands, appears on the side of the Violet Crown Cinema building.

The *I Love Charlottesville A Lot* mural is iconic. Frequently photographed and the backdrop of thousands of visitor selfies, the artwork is on the side of an automotive shop in Belmont. The O's in the words are used tires.

The *Charlottesville Bikes* mural appears on the concrete wall that lines the walkway on West Market Street.

charlottesvillemuralproject.org

ROW YOUR BOAT
ON THE RIVANNA RESERVOIR

Anyone who has tried a rowing machine at the gym knows that rowing is a great workout. Rowing in the water is even better. You can learn to row the right way in beautiful surroundings on the Rivanna Reservoir. The Rivanna Rowing Club offers a variety of programs, from the beginner-targeted Learn-to-Row classes to personal coaching for the seasoned sculling team. Early risers will like getting out on the water before work; others will prefer the late afternoon classes. Everyone, however, will get into shape. Programs are available for junior rowers (13 to 18 years of age) and adults. Boats and equipment provided.

rivannarowing.org

TIP

The Rowing Club hosts an annual regatta in the late summer, so training can pay off in a friendly competition. A potluck picnic follows the race.

CHEER FOR THE 'HOOS,
NO MATTER YOUR SPORT

The University of Virginia offers more than just world-class education. You may have heard of its sports teams as well, famous for football, basketball, baseball, field hockey, golf, tennis, squash, and much, much more! Pick your sport, buy your tickets, and be a fan. In Charlottesville, we call our fans and the athletes Wahoos—or 'Hoos for short—at UVA. Officially, UVA's mascot and teams are the Cavaliers, but at games, the customary yell is "Wahoowa!" Wear blue and orange and you'll fit right in.

virginiasports.com

TIP

If you're having trouble getting your hands on sometimes costly tickets for men's sporting events, check out the women's teams, where the talent and competition are just as hot.

CAMP OR GLAMP
IN THE GREAT OUTDOORS

Camping is, admittedly, not for everyone. If it's your bag, however, Central Virginia is a great place to do it. Our weather is mild enough that there's easily three full seasons of comfortable camping with the right gear. RV camping, cabin camping, and full-on glamping (a.k.a. glamorous camping with every amenity a camper can have) are also available at several campgrounds in the region.

Misty Mountain Camp Resort is great for families and allows for a downright affordable staycation. The resort is great for RVs or tents and offers a pool, a spray park, ziplines, canoe and kayak rental, wine and brewery tours, and all the outdoor amenities your camping heart desires.

Camping spots are plentiful in Shenandoah National Park, naturally, and backcountry camping is available by permit for the truly adventurous. If you're the tamer type, look into the four campgrounds with various options: Mathews Arm, Big Meadows, Lewis Mountain, and Loft Mountain. All have access to well-maintained hiking trails with visits to spectacular waterfalls. For the comfort camper, look into a stay at the Big Meadows Lodge or a cabin at Skyland Resort, and enjoy the historic surroundings in style.

Places to Camp

Misty Mountain Camp Resort
56 Misty Mountain Rd., Greenwood, 540-456-6409
mistymountaincampresort.com

Shenandoah National Park
3655 E. Hwy. 211, Luray, 540-999-3500
goshenandoah.com

SNUGGLE A BABY GOAT
AT CAROMONT FARM

Sometimes all a baby goat needs is a snuggle. Gail Hobbs-Page runs a goat dairy and cheese-making operation at Caromont Farm, where more than 30,000 pounds of cheese per year is produced. Good cheese happens when goats are happy. To socialize baby goats and prepare them for milking, Gail asks for visitors to take tours, learn about and buy her delicious cheese, and yes, snuggle the goats. Gail's original call for goat cuddlers went viral, causing an overwhelming influx of volunteers. Now, the planned snuggle sessions sell out far in advance. We highly recommend the experience; adorable baby goat antics will put a smile on your face, and Gail's selection of award-winning cheeses will likely fill your tummy and your takeaway bag.

9261 Old Green Mountain Rd., Esmont, 434-831-1393
caromontcheese.com

EXPLORE ROUND TOP
AT FOXHAVEN FARM

At the intersection of Reservoir Road and Foxhaven Farm Road is a 280-acre treasure well worth exploring. Foxhaven Farm, with its vast fields, wide trails, wooded mountain climbs, and pine forests, is a gorgeous place to spend a day. Choose the trails that go up to Round Top, a ridge overlooking the Boar's Head property and Birdwood Golf Course, or stick to the flatter walkways around the fields for easier strolls.

Foxhaven Farm and the Round Top hike are both dog-friendly. Signs with boars on them do not warn of wild boars in the area but rather serve as trail markers for guests of the Boar's Head Resort to follow.

Once the property of garden and hiking enthusiast Jane Heyward, most of the land is now owned by the University of Virginia Foundation. The beloved former resident's private property, including a home and several outbuildings, is found at the end of the Foxhaven Farm driveway. Enter the property from Reservoir Road and park in the small lot to the left. Trails begin in the field to the left of the parking area. Or, continue down the side of Foxhaven Farm Road until you reach the Jane Heyward Gardens on the right. Review the map before you explore the gardens to avoid trespassing at the private residence there. A springtime visit reveals a carpet of Lenten roses and periwinkle.

boarsheadresort.com

HIT THE LINKS
AT A LOCAL GOLF COURSE

Full Cry at Keswick, Meadowcreek, Birdwood, Spring Creek, Farmington, Old Trail, and Glenmore—what are these hifalutin-sounding names? Why, golf courses, of course! Our greens are great, and golf enthusiasts love to get out and play 18 holes whenever weather permits. A few are private (Glenmore, Full Cry at Keswick, Farmington), so you'll have to find a member to let you play, but the rest are public, so step on up to the tee and swing away.

Check Out These Golf Courses

Full Cry at Keswick
701 Club Dr., Keswick, 434-923-4363
keswick.com

Meadowcreek Golf Course
1400 Pen Park Rd., 434-977-0615
meadowcreekgolf.org

Birdwood Golf Course
410 Golf Course Dr., 434-293-4653
boarsheadinn.com/golf

Spring Creek Golf Club
109 Clubhouse Way, Zion Crossroads, 540-832-0744
springcreekgolfclub.com

Farmington Country Club
1625 Country Club Cir., 434-296-5661
farmingtoncc.com

Old Trail Golf Club
5494 Golf Dr., Crozet, 434-823-8101
oldtrailgolf.com

The Club at Glenmore
1750 Piper Way, 434-977-0701
theclubatglenmore.com

CRUISE SKYLINE DRIVE
TO SEE STUNNING VIEWS

The finest views of the Shenandoah Valley are displayed with breathtaking vistas best viewed from along Skyline Drive. This 105-mile route winds through central Virginia from Front Royal to Rockfish Gap and is one of the most spectacular ways to enjoy the fall foliage or the spring bloom. A meticulously planned roadway, Skyline Drive has 75 overlooks. Pack a picnic and plan to relax and enjoy several stops along the journey.

visitskylinedrive.org

TIP
Skyline Drive is often closed for inclement weather in the winter. Fog can make travel extremely dangerous throughout the year. Pay attention to road conditions before you set out on a Skyline trip. It's easier to see the views if the sky and the roads are clear.

VISIT SHENANDOAH NATIONAL PARK
FOR OUTDOOR ADVENTURE

There are so very many reasons to visit Shenandoah National Park. Hiking, camping, exploring, spelunking, and nature watching are just some of the ways to spend time in the park. Catch a glimpse of black bears, deer, reptiles, amphibians, birds, and more. People have lived in the region of the park for more than 9,000 years, but the park itself was created between 1933 and 1942 as a project of Franklin Delano Roosevelt's Civilian Conservation Corps.

SNP has a huge network of trails with waterfalls, swimming holes, and mountain peaks. You might meet some long-distance hikers on the trails; the park includes a section of the Appalachian Trail, which extends from Maine to Georgia.

3655 E Hwy. 211, Luray, 540-999-3500
nps.gov/shen

LEARN TO SALSA
WITH ZABOR DANCE

Edwin Roa is the founder of Zabor Dance and the instigator behind Charlottesville Salsa Club. To generate interest from beginners, Roa began hosting two weekly parties: Sundays for salsa and Wednesdays for bachata fusion. Bachata, which originated in the 1950s in the Dominican Republic, is a sensual dance that has gone mainstream. It is slower than salsa and similar to bolero and merengue.

The club starts each party with a lesson, making sure the environment is welcoming for all beginners. Then the more seasoned dancers hit their strides and really show off their moves. Come as a spectator, and you may find that your feet make the decision to join in for you!

If the salsa club dance parties really pique your interest, sign up for regular lessons through Zabor Dance, and get ready to sweep local competitions.

109 2nd St. SE, 434-270-0699
zabordance.com

ROLE-PLAY
IN DARDEN TOWE PARK

Live action role-playing, otherwise known as LARPing, is known to a small subsection of people who are enthusiastic about outdoor recreation, storytelling, and, yes, combat. In Charlottesville, that group is Zorn Vongal, a family-focused medieval-style battle game set in the Dark Ages. Think of the J. R. R. Tolkien *Lord of the Rings* trilogy come to life.

Zorn Vongal is a member organization with about 40 participants engaging in full contact combat with buffer weapons. Every Sunday, the group hosts battle and training exercises at Darden Towe Park from noon until around 5 p.m.

The battles are not for the faint of heart, with fiberglass weapons buffered with foam and fabric to cause only minor damage—bruises, but no broken bones or skin. That being said, the organization is focused on health and safety while providing physically rigorous activity that contributes to storylines and supports mental health. The games focus on honor, integrity, sportsmanship, and teamwork.

If participation isn't your bag, Zorn Vongal enthusiastically welcomes spectators, with a marked section just for the interested audience.

zornvongal.com

GET BOWLED OVER
AT BOWLERO

Go bowling at Bowlero/AMF Kegler's Lanes for a date, with the family, or with a group. One of the great things about living in a small town is that there's no confusion when you say to friends, "Meet me at the bowling alley!" Bowlero is north on I-29 in Albemarle County, and luckily for bowling enthusiasts all over the region, they do it right. There's plenty of space, with 48 lanes, a billiards room, video games, and a lounge. It's great for parties or a rainy afternoon with the kids, and it's friendly to everyone from very serious league bowlers to the totally casual bowler (that's me).

If you're looking for an indoor venue for a corporate event, Bowlero has a full menu of party platters and drink specials to make your event planning a snap.

335 Rivanna Plaza Dr., 434-978-3999
amf.com/keglerslanes

GO FISH
WITH ALBEMARLE ANGLER

There's plenty of good fishing to be done in the mountain streams of Virginia. Make sure you catch some by engaging an expert. Local outfit Albemarle Angler has experienced fly-fishing guides who know the area's waterways, best techniques, equipment, and the secret hangouts of aquatic friends. A guided fishing excursion with Albemarle Angler provides access to some of the best private water around. Whether on your own or with a guide, you'll need a fishing license—we don't let just anyone catch our swimming dinners.

1129 Emmet St. N, 434-977-6882
albemarleangler.com

TIP
If fishing is your thing, consider a Sachem's Pass membership, entitling you to private water access, special events, guided fishing trips, specialized equipment, and an in-store discount.

GET TUBULAR
WITH JAMES RIVER RUNNERS

Tubing on the James River is a summertime tradition—but not one for the faint of heart. I've canoed and kayaked, white water rafted and sailed. Nothing, however, compares to the lazy living that is floating in a tube down the James River. It is one part cultural spectacle, one part nature appreciation, and one part shenanigan. The requirements for a successful tubing day include an early start and a stockpile of your favorite beer in a cooler with snacks, sandwiches, and whatever other provisions you'll need to sustain you for a five-mile float downriver.

Do yourself a favor and engage James River Runners. They'll take you upriver by bus and provide life vests, tubes, and guidance for a successful river floating experience.

10092 Hatton Ferry Rd., Scottsville, 434-286-2338
facebook.com/jamesriverrunners

TIP

The cultural spectacle includes
fellow floaters in a variety of swim
attire and with a range of capacity for
adult beverages (most consumed on the
water in the form of cans of beer or vodka-
infused Jell-O shots). You'll see a variety of
questionable behaviors on the float downriver,
so think carefully about whether you make this
trip a family event. Drunken shenanigans are
a standard feature on the float, and if your
tolerance for foul language, beer swilling,
and tattoos is low, you might want to
stay on dry land.

CULTURE AND HISTORY

HONOR
THE ENSLAVED LABORERS
AT THE UNIVERSITY OF VIRGINIA

In 2020, the Memorial to Enslaved Laborers was completed on the grounds of UVA. The structure represents the 4,000 to 5,000 enslaved people who lived and worked at UVA at some point between 1817 and 1865. Each name or listing represents a person who performed a task to build or maintain the university or to serve its students and professors. There were 4,000 known enslaved community members, but full names are known for fewer than 600. Historians continue to work to discover the remaining names to add to the memorial.

Among the work done, enslaved people cleared land, dug foundations, and built all of the buildings—work that included highly skilled labor such as carpentry, brickmaking, roofing, stone carving, blacksmithing, and more. Daily tasks—including fetching water, chopping and stacking wood, cooking, cleaning, making clothing, and generally seeing to the needs of an entire community—fell to these unpaid and mistreated men, women, and children.

The monument is both beautiful and moving, an oasis for peace and reflection. The continued work to add names creates an ever-evolving, ongoing examination of the true history of the university.

slavery.virginia.edu/memorial-for-enslaved-laborers

ATTEND A HISTORY DINNER
AT INDIGO HOUSE

Imagine sitting down to a home-cooked dinner and learning each dish's history, from the author of the recipe and their culture, cooking methods, and way of life to the way the ingredients were grown, raised, and prepared.

Dr. Leni Sorensen is a food historian, farmer, gardener, cook, and epic storyteller. Not only that, but she's a folk singer who appeared as part of the group the Womenfolk on the *Ed Sullivan Show*—three times! Sorensen grows, prepares, and preserves most of her own food. A seat at her kitchen table or a spot at her counter, while learning to can peaches and tomatoes or to make tamales, is an unforgettable experience.

Sorensen opens her home, Indigo House, to guests for what she calls "history dinners." The dinners feature food grown on the five-acre property and prepared using cookbooks from the 1700s and 1800s, all with stories of their own. Featured in the Netflix special *High on the Hog*, Sorensen is one of a few food historians who devote themselves to teaching and cooking for the public.

indigohouse.us

EXERCISE YOUR RIGHT
TO FREEDOM OF SPEECH

Write something thoughtful or crazy on the Community Chalkboard, a public landmark and monument to the First Amendment on the Pavilion end of the Downtown Mall. Declare your unrequited love. Scrawl song lyrics. Draw a funny or serious picture. Take time to read what others have written. Be inspired, moved, offended, or amused. Then come back again in a week or so and read, write, or draw something entirely different. (The monument is "refreshed" twice a week.) The wall is a common meeting spot and the backdrop for protests and demonstrations.

In 2021, the lease on the wall was taken over by the Bridge Progressive Arts Initiative. Fundraising to support maintenance and repair to the wall is underway through the Charlottesville Area Community Foundation. Hopefully the wall will continue to serve the community for generations to come.

The east end of the Downtown Mall near City Hall
thebridgepai.org

READ SOME POE
AND SEE HIS DORM ROOM AT UVA

Pick up a book of Edgar Allan Poe's; I recommend anything including his poems "The Raven" or "Annabel Lee." Take it with you to the sealed room appointed and preserved by the honorary Raven Society on the Grounds of the University of Virginia where the poet may have lived in 1826. (It's possible his actual room was another similar room nearby.) Poe was a student at the university for just one year. Two of his works, "Tamerlane" and "A Tale of the Ragged Mountains," refer to his experiences in Charlottesville. Conduct a live reading of one of your favorite works, either with or without an audience.

McCormick Road
UVA Grounds, West Range #13

NOTE

The bed in the room is the one Poe slept in while living with his foster parents in Richmond. Poe's middle name, Allan, comes from the surname of his foster family.

LET THERE BE LIGHT
AT PIEDMONT VIRGINIA COMMUNITY COLLEGE

Each year around the holiday season, the grounds of Piedmont Virginia Community College transform at night into an interactive art exhibit. Let There Be Light is a collaboration among several area artists working with light as a medium. Some exhibits are elaborate still works; others include dancers with light-up costumes. A self-guided tour of ethereal, magical creations meant to be seen in the dark, the whole exhibition is available as a walk- or drive-through experience.

Contributing artists are well-known local people, student groups, and performers. It's exciting to see how different each exhibit is and how many there are from year to year.

A local favorite nighttime, outdoor winter event, Let There Be Light attracts many neighbors and friends, celebrating art and light together. The event is free, open to the public, and family-friendly.

501 College Dr., 434-977-6918
lettherebelightpvcc.com

EXPLORE BLACK HISTORY
AT THE JEFFERSON SCHOOL AFRICAN AMERICAN HERITAGE CENTER

The Jefferson School City Center was once a high school for Black students in Charlottesville, established in 1926. Today, the building houses the African American Heritage Center, a collection of historical exhibits and a center for education and special events. Visitors can attend lectures and enjoy concerts and films. The Isabella Gibbons Local History Center, on-site at the Jefferson School, is a rich resource for those interested in local history and genealogy, with an archive of more than 60 oral histories of students who attended the school between 1930 and 1960.

233 4th St. NW, 434-260-8720
jeffschoolheritagecenter.org

TIP
Book a tour in advance for $5 per adult and add the experience of a guided look at the historic building, the exhibits, and a selection of educational activities.

MEET A WRITER
AT THE VIRGINIA FESTIVAL OF THE BOOK

The Festival of the Book, a program of Virginia Humanities, has something for all readers. The festival lasts five days and attracts readers and writers from all over the Commonwealth. Highlights include a business breakfast keynoted by a well-known author; small sessions for aspiring crime-fiction writers, biographers, romance novelists, and the like; and a kids' fair. Charlottesville is full of bookstores, writers, and readers, among them John Grisham, John Hart, Rita Mae Brown, Kathryn Erskine, and more. Spot a famous writer at the festival, or hear one speak! Book signings abound, so bring your book allowance and be prepared to stock up.

vabook.org

SEE THE LIGHTS OF KEY WEST
DURING THE HOLIDAYS

Key West really lights it up for the holidays. Not only do the homeowners really get on board with lights and inflatables, Griswold-style, but they also line the streets with luminaria—you know, what used to be paper bags filled with sand and glowing with a lit candle inside. Nowadays, the bags are often plastic and the lights electric, but the effect is the same (and safer). It's a beautiful sight to behold, particularly if we're lucky enough to score a white Christmas. Take a walk, not just a drive, through the neighborhood to get the full impact of the scene. The Key West neighborhood is located one mile north of Charlottesville on VA Route 20. An interesting history lesson: the land is the west side of the property granted to a man named Martin Key in 1731 by King George II of England.

keywestassociation.org

DIG UP
A LITERARY TREASURE
AT THE UNIVERSITY OF VIRGINIA LIBRARY

Alderman Library at the University of Virginia boasts five million books and journals from around the world. With a Virginia resident ID, you can check out books. If you're from elsewhere, you're welcome to read and research on-site.

If that's not enough to whet your bibliophile appetite, check out the Albert and Shirley Small Special Collections Library. The Small Library features more than 16 million objects, including manuscripts, archival records, rare books, maps, broadsides, photographs, audio and video recordings, and more. It's a seriously cool exhibit for anyone with a love of literature and history.

UVA Library
2450 Old Ivy Rd., 434-924-3021
library.virginia.edu

Albert and Shirley Small Special Collections Library
170 McCormick Rd., 434-243-1776
small.library.virginia.edu

BLESS THE HOUNDS
AT GRACE EPISCOPAL CHURCH

A very sweet—and very typically Charlottesville—tradition is more than 80 years old and takes place every Thanksgiving morning. The Blessing of the Hounds is a special gathering at Grace Episcopal Church in the community of Keswick. Since 1929, the church has cleverly enticed fox hunters to come to church on Thanksgiving morning, offering special blessings for their hunting dogs and horses. In the oldest ceremony of its kind in the United States, more than a thousand people come to witness the Keswick Hunt Club dogs receive their blessing. If you're a dog or horse lover and want a special way to kick off Thanksgiving, this is it.

5607 Gordonsville Rd., Keswick, 434-293-3549
gracekeswick.org

TIP

For those interested in the rich history of the region, the church grounds feature a large graveyard where members of Virginia's oldest families are interred. There are 110 known veterans from the Civil War through the Vietnam War buried there, and the church provides a guide to enable visitors to pay their respects.

HONE YOUR CRAFT
AT WRITERHOUSE

WriterHouse is an unbelievably rich resource for the wannabe writer as well as those who have already published. WriterHouse is both a location and an organization, providing space for writers to work, undistracted and free from coffeehouse patrons or well-intentioned friends and family members. It's also a collection of programs and classes for all levels of writing expertise and for various writing disciplines. In addition, it's a place where writers can gather and meet to help one another through critique groups, mentoring, readings, and other events. It's the place for writers: a home away from home and a room of one's own. Join, write, teach, learn, or just visit.

508 Dale Ave., 434-282-6643
writerhouse.org

NOTE

Charlottesville seems to be a haven for authors. At last count, there were at least 50. Notables include Rita Dove, Rita Mae Brown, Jocelyn Nicole Johnson, Kathryn Erskine, John Grisham, and John Hart.

TAKE A TREK
TO PINE KNOT

In southern Albemarle County, visitors can find the wooded retreat of Theodore and Edith Roosevelt. The property is called Pine Knot and hosted the president, his wife, and their children when they needed a vacation getaway from May 1905 to May 1908. The rustic, two-story dwelling with its deep front porch remains unchanged from that time.

It's easy to imagine Teddy Roosevelt hiking, hunting, and birdwatching in the surrounding woods. It's difficult to imagine any modern president's family choosing the totally unfinished cabin with its utter lack of amenities as a relaxing retreat. Although, what better way to get away from it all than a cabin in the woods with no running water, electricity, or internet?

Today the cabin is maintained by the Edith and Theodore Roosevelt Pine Knot Foundation, and you can visit it if you make an appointment.

Scottsville, 434-286-6106
pineknot.org

EXPLORE HISTORY ON FOOT
IN COURT SQUARE

A collection of notable historic landmarks sits in Court Square in the heart of the city. The building at 300 Court Square is a brick replacement of the Eagle Tavern, a wood frame building that stood there in 1791. It was used as the headquarters of Federal occupying forces after the Civil War.

At "0" Court Square is the site of Charlottesville's slave auction block. The Slave Auction Block Marker is a monument that has been repeatedly stolen and replaced by the city. The building was built in the 1820s in Jeffersonian style. Down the adjacent Sixth Street, the historic buildings once housed merchant supplies, a small library, a whiskey dealer, and a Swiss watchmaker recruited by Thomas Jefferson himself.

Other buildings of note in the Square include the former Swan Tavern at 300 Park Street, made famous by Revolutionary hero Jack Jouett, whose father owned the Swan. 350 Park Street was once the Town Hall, then the Levy Opera House. Guests can visit the Albemarle Charlottesville Historical Society to learn more about Court Square and other historical sites and to sign up for walking tours of the downtown area, which is full of opportunities to explore the past.

Albemarle Charlottesville Historical Society
200 2nd St. NE, 434-296-1492
albemarlehistory.org

BE INSPIRED
AT THE MCGUFFEY ART CENTER

The McGuffey School was built in 1916 and, in 1975, was reborn as an art center. Classrooms were converted into airy, spacious art studios, and three galleries provide the largest art display space in Charlottesville. More than 45 artists rent space at McGuffey, but the organization has well over 150 members who display art in the galleries and participate in events. Every first Friday of the month is a new gallery opening, and when the art center is open, so is the gift shop, so you can take home your own piece of locally created art.

201 2nd St. NW, 434-295-7973
mcguffeyartcenter.com

NOTE
McGuffey offers a residency program that provides, upon application approval, free studio space for up to two months to artists who qualify.

VISIT THREE PRESIDENTS' HOMES:
MONTPELIER, HIGHLAND, AND MONTICELLO

Thomas Jefferson's Monticello gets all the attention. Don't skip out on seeing the other two presidents' homes in the region, however. A short distance away—in Orange, Virginia—Montpelier was the home of James and Dolley Madison. The restored home is an interactive, educational experience, and the gardens are majestic to behold. The slave quarters, whose recent reconstruction is the work of more than two decades of archaeology on the property, tell a more in-depth story of our nation's history.

Highland, the occasional residence of James Monroe, is practically spitting distance from Monticello. Although the original house where Monroe lived was destroyed in a fire, the estate's history and ongoing story are of interest. The trails on the grounds are excellent—well-maintained and scenic.

Anyone who has ever been to Charlottesville will tell you to visit Thomas Jefferson's home at Monticello. It's Charlottesville's main attraction: the home designed by the father of the University of Virginia, the principal author of the Declaration of Independence, and the third president of the United States. The best way to experience Monticello is with an Evening Signature tour. This exclusive-access pass will give you an expert's tour of the remarkable gardens and the off-limits third-floor Dome Room. Even the most casual gardener will be fascinated by the history, planning, and cultivation of the plantation's self-sustaining gardens.

James Madison's Montpelier
13384 Laundry Rd., Montpelier Station, 540-672-2728
montpelier.org

James Monroe's Highland
2050 James Monroe Pkwy., 434-293-8000
ashlawnhighland.org

Thomas Jefferson's Monticello
931 Thomas Jefferson Pkwy., 434-984-9800
monticello.org

TIPS

The Fourth of July is Monticello's big day. The US Citizens' Naturalization Ceremony is a highlight and features an impressive speaker, along with an incredibly moving ceremony that will give any American a dose of patriotic pride. Locals who can prove with an ID that they live in Charlottesville can get in for free when bringing a guest.

APPRECIATE
THE CONTEMPORARY
AT SECOND STREET GALLERY

Second Street Gallery, a block off the Downtown Mall on Water Street, is the oldest contemporary art space in central Virginia. Founded in 1973, the gallery features regularly rotating exhibitions of local and traveling artists. Hosting around 14 exhibitions each year, the gallery is active in its outreach and curation of contemporary art.

A themed exhibition that in 2021 was in its fourth iteration is the Teeny Tiny Trifecta. This group exhibition invites artists to submit three small works of art each. The art in the exhibition is in a range of styles, techniques, and media, all with one common attribute: each is a nine-by-nine-inch or smaller work of art.

Second Street Gallery is a favorite place to spend an afternoon browsing for a new piece to enhance your living space. Watch for announcements about exhibition openings, evening events for special gatherings, and meet-the-artist events.

115 2nd St. SE, 434-977-7284
secondstreetgallery.org

GET
AN ARTIST'S EDUCATION
AT THE FRALIN

The Fralin Museum of Art at the University of Virginia is a short walk away from the Rotunda on the University Grounds. The museum has an impressive permanent collection of over 14,000 works, including African and Native American art, American and European painting, photography, and works on paper. Used as a teaching museum for academic departments at the university, the Fralin also hosts community and school groups through outreach programs.

New exhibitions appear quarterly. In the past, the museum hosted The Unexpected O'Keeffe, a celebration of the era in which artist Georgia O'Keeffe attended the university. Her watercolors and other paintings of the time, including her works of sites around Charlottesville, such as the Rotunda, were displayed in the exhibit.

Admission is free, and the museum is open to the public.

155 Rugby Rd., 434-924-3592
uvafralinartmuseum.virginia.edu

PLAY INDOORS
AT VIRGINIA DISCOVERY MUSEUM

An indoor playland with hours of learning disguised as fun, the Virginia Discovery Museum is a great experience for little people. A pint-sized C'ville has a restaurant, a post office, and a theater to inspire hours of pretend play. The Discovery Museum encourages family play, so no break for parents—get down on the floor and play right along with the young ones.

524 E Main St., 434-977-1025
vadm.org

TIP

Explore the Discovery Museum's seasonal educational programs, or sign the kids up to learn to play chess. Living Lab, an optional science-based program, enables children to be active participants in a research project with Child Development Labs at UVA.

BE LOCALLY, SOCIALLY AWARE

In the summer of 2017, Charlottesville was the site of the largest to date recorded gathering of white supremacists. Heather Heyer, an anti-racism activist, was killed when a white nationalist rally participant drove his car into the crowd, injuring many others. Fourth Street NE, the site of the tragedy, has been renamed with signage declaring it Heather Heyer Way. The section of sidewalk often has chalk drawings, flowers, candles, and other mementos honoring Heyer. Stop by, pay your respects, and think about the role racism plays, not just in Charlottesville, but in our country, and consider what we can do to effect change. As Heyer said in her final Facebook post before her death, "If you're not outraged, you're not paying attention."

If you're a local resident, get involved in area nonprofits, join a committee, get to know your neighbors, or run for local office.

SEE A TRULY SPECTACULAR TREE
ON THE GROUNDS AT UVA

You might think that seeing one particular tree wouldn't make a list of this kind, but this isn't just any tree. Found on the west side of the Rotunda on UVA's Grounds, this ginkgo tree was planted in 1860 by UVA's first superintendent, William Pratt. Known as the "Pratt Ginkgo," this majestic tree turns color late in fall, then drops its leaves practically all at once, carpeting the ground beneath with golden leaves. It is the universal sign, at the university, that winter has come.

NOTE

Some people associate ginkgoes with an unpleasant odor. Female ginkgoes do produce seeds that have a particularly distinctive smell; male ginkgoes do not. The Pratt Ginkgo is a male tree.

VIEW AN ABORIGINAL ART COLLECTION
AT THE KLUGE-RUHE

The Kluge-Ruhe Aboriginal Art Collection of the University of Virginia is the only museum in the United States dedicated to the exhibition and study of Australian Aboriginal art. The museum features the art and culture of Australia's indigenous people.

The Kluge-Ruhe Collection opened in 1997 through a gift by Charlottesville businessman John W. Kluge (1914–2010). In the late 1980s and 1990s, Kluge compiled one of the finest private collections of Australian Aboriginal art in the world. Today, the collection includes acrylic paintings, blown glass, installations, drawings, photographs, and more. It's the only collection of its kind, and it's right here in Charlottesville.

400 Worrell Dr., 434-244-0234
kluge-ruhe.org

STARGAZE
AT MCCORMICK OBSERVATORY

On Friday nights, the McCormick Observatory at the University of Virginia Department of Astronomy opens to the public. Get a chance to observe the stars and planets through the McCormick and Fan Mountain telescopes. Weather permitting (clouds tend to get in the way of stargazing), guests are invited to peek at the sky through all the facility's telescopes, experience audio-visual presentations, see the museum exhibits, and tour the observatory. Faculty, post-doctoral candidates, and graduate students host and answer questions. It's great as an outing for a group, a date, or a family night. Call ahead.

600 McCormick Rd., 434-924-7494
astronomy.as.virginia.edu

NOTE
Leander McCormick, for whom the observatory is named due to his donation of the telescope, was the brother of Cyrus McCormick, who is credited with the invention of the mechanical reaper. It was, in fact, their father, Robert McCormick, who invented the reaper. Cyrus patented it and founded International Harvester.

GO TRICK-OR-TREATING
ON THE LAWN AT UVA

Easily the cutest sight of the year, children are invited to trick-or-treat at the doors of the 54 student rooms that line the University of Virginia Lawn (and are traditionally awarded as residences to top students). More than 70 student-run organizations donate candy to be dispensed to cherubs in costume. The event happens every Halloween from 4 p.m. to 6 p.m. and is a great defined way to safely usher young children through their first door-to-door Halloween experience. For parents, it's a delightful way to see the community in costume and hobnob with friends while little ones play and collect their goodies. It's a pretty great town-plus-gown event and a nice way to spend some time on the Grounds as a guest.

NOTE

It is one of UVA's highest honors: being chosen for residence in one of the student rooms on the Lawn. Famous Lawn residents have included Katie Couric and Edgar Allan Poe.

SHOPPING AND FASHION

EARN A MASTER'S IN MANGA
AT TELEGRAPH

Browse Telegraph Art & Comics' tiny Downtown Mall location for manga (comics of Japanese origin) and comic fans' greatest hits. The store offers collectibles and board games and is an excellent spot to shop for the teen or pre-teen in your life. And if you were going to attempt to earn a master's degree in manga, Telegraph would be a very good place to start.

Enthusiasts will find favorite comics, graphic novels, and artwork in the downtown shop. Up north, in Telegraph's Seminole Square store, the much larger storefront allows for browsing bins of comic collections, gatherings of collectors, and game sales.

Telegraph is more than a retail outlet owned by a local family; it's a hub for like-minded folks to gather and share their passion for role-playing games, art, and literature. Come find a collectible treasure, a favorite read, and your people.

211 W Main St., 434-244-3210
398 Hillsdale Dr., 434-974-7512

telegraphcomics.com

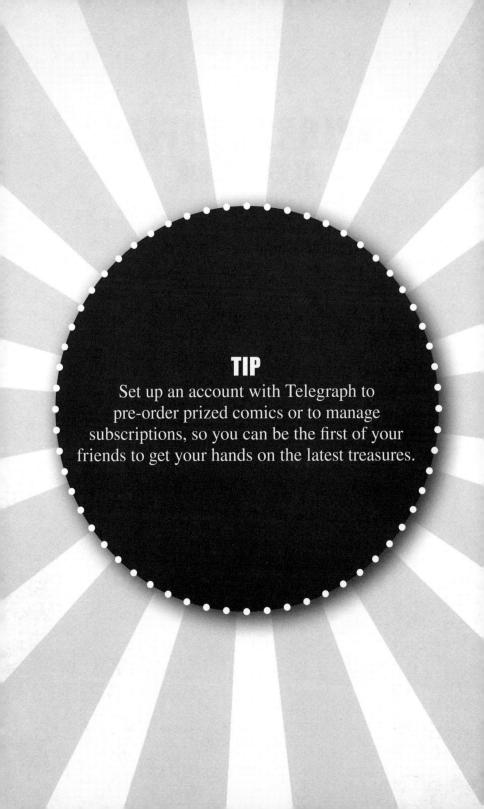

TIP

Set up an account with Telegraph to pre-order prized comics or to manage subscriptions, so you can be the first of your friends to get your hands on the latest treasures.

EXPLORE AND PLAY
AT ALAKAZAM

Alakazam is different from every toy store and toy department we've ever experienced. It's a carefully curated collection of items for children of all ages. The owners consider five factors when choosing items to add to their shelves: toys that are well-designed, playable, affordable, inclusive, and made well fill the store.

The chalkboard riddle outside the store on the Downtown Mall is what often stumps potential customers enough to venture inside. Once past the door, no one can resist a browse—or even a purchase—in the inviting, welcoming store. The store's owner, the perfectly named Ellen Joy, took over the store in 2019 with big plans to update and serve a bustling downtown location. Fully renovated in 2021, Alakazam is the ideal stop on the way to a gift-giving event, as the staff will cheerfully wrap your purchase before sending you on your way.

100 E Main St., 434-971-1717
alakazamtoys.com

TREAT YOUR FEET
AT RAGGED MOUNTAIN RUNNING SHOP

Central Virginia provides numerous opportunities to get out and move your feet. Whether running is your speed or you prefer a walk, Ragged Mountain Running Shop is the place locals go to measure feet, learn about gait, and get fitted with the perfect footwear. It is a family-owned business, and the Lorenzonis are fitness fixtures in our community. They give back through community engagement and charitable donations and with care and excellence in customer service. Local deliveries are speedy and come with a handwritten thank you note. Purchase records are meticulously kept so customers can replace footwear easily when they've put as many miles as they can on their current pair.

Located a step back from the Corner at the University of Virginia, the shop has its own convenient parking, but you'll get bonus points if you run or walk there.

Among Mark Lorenzoni's valuable guidance to walkers and runners, which he provides regularly on social media and in partnership with charitable organizations throughout the region, is a map of the best streets on which to view holiday lights in the city in November and December. Mark's thorough investigation of Charlottesville's lit-up yard game will give your family the perfect route to take the kids on a snowy night drive that will delight folks of all ages.

3 Elliewood Ave., 434-293-3367
raggedmountainrunning.com

FIND GREAT JUNK
AT AN ECLECTIC RESALE SHOP

In college, my friend Ellen was fond of "going junking," the term she applied to long Saturdays spent exploring consignment and used goods stores. These abound in the Commonwealth, from the upscale to the rare antique collection to the battered, truly used "junk." Replenished frequently by transient students and academics, great finds are available year-round but particularly in the early summer, when there's high turnover among the resident population. Keep an eye out for incredible vintage clothing and collectible works of art.

There are treasures out there for anyone. Some favorite stops for eclectic shopping are listed here.

EAT FROM A TREE
WHILE YOU SHOP
AT EDIBLE LANDSCAPING

Edible Landscaping is not merely a landscaping store; rather, it's a Garden of Eden on the outskirts of Charlottesville. Wander the rows of fragrant flowering fruit trees and explore varieties of plants and shrubs you've never considered. Learn what grows well in this climate and what you shouldn't bother planting. Don't eat lunch before you go in the summertime; instead, stroll around and sample blueberries, strawberries, apples, and peaches from their source. You'll be entranced and, if you're not already, convinced that you, too, can be a farmer. Come to learn and to buy; prepare to be enchanted.

361 Spirit Ridge Ln., Afton, 434-361-9134
ediblelandscaping.com

TIP
Watch for three annual events: All About Fruit, Persimmon Festival, and Fall Fruit Festival, a chance to learn, taste, and explore.

TURN A PAGE
AT NEW DOMINION BOOKSHOP

New Dominion Bookshop is the oldest bookstore in the Commonwealth of Virginia and is known for its exemplary customer service and cozy atmosphere. Staff recommendations and new release events have gained the bookshop a loyal following.

Inside the shop, a grand staircase leads to a second-story stage, perfect for small author events, readings, and book clubs. The light streaming in from the second-floor windows creates an excellent atmosphere for browsing. With more than 20,000 books in the shop, there's a good read for every taste.

Guests who visit in the springtime will find a glorious secret rose garden through the store and out the back door, walled in by the brick buildings on either side and a chain protecting it from the alley beyond. In late May, the blooms fill an archway above, and guests are permitted to bring a lunch and sit among the rose petals.

Follow the bookshop online to stay alert to Rose Garden Days when the garden is in full bloom. Looking for a special tiny wedding venue for you and your fellow beloved bookhound? This garden is open to event bookings.

404 E Main St., 434-295-2552
ndbookshop.com

MAKE YOUR OWN WARDROBE
AT EWE

Part shop, part studio, EWE (like the lady sheep) offers a carefully curated selection of fabrics, yarns, patterns, and notions for eager knitters and sewers. Guided knitting and sewing classes will help even the most inexperienced student get started. The sewing studio gives students access to machines at an hourly rate.

Have you ever fantasized about creating your own capsule wardrobe? EWE classes offer guidance from people who have done just that. Follow the store's Instagram to see shop employees and students modeling their own creations for inspiration to get started.

Committed to diversity and inclusion, EWE strives to be a welcoming environment for people who come together through fiber arts and support. Started from a desire to source great knitting and sewing products for the community, the EWE group has made its mark in Charlottesville. If you're looking for a nurturing, supportive group to knit with or for help with a sewing project that's got you stuck, look no further than the EWE studio.

617 W Main St., 434-409-9095
ewefibers.com

SHOP LOCAL
AT C'VILLE ARTS COOPERATIVE GALLERY

The C'ville Arts storefront on the Downtown Mall has long been marked by a colorful mosaic loveseat. Central to the Mall, find inside the engaging shop window a collective representing more than 60 local artists!

C'ville Arts is a great place to shop for all types of art and crafts. Find jewelry, prints, photography, ceramics, leatherworks, and more. It's the perfect spot to find unique gifts, special artwork to decorate your walls, or just a little something to treat yourself.

Supporting local businesses—and especially local artists— is a big part of Charlottesville culture, and the C'ville Arts shop is a perfect way to immerse yourself in it.

118 E Main St., 434-972-9500
cvillearts.org

TIP
As a cooperative venture, member artists staff the store, helping keep costs low and providing shoppers the chance to meet an artist in person!

• •

PAINT A PLATE
AT LAZY DAISY

A great rainy-day activity or a good group playdate for kids or grownups, painting pottery is fun, relaxing, and occasionally productive! Our friends have been crafting an eclectic collection of dessert plates, made two at a time and with no two the same. Kids love the creativity involved in choosing a pottery piece; selecting stencils, colors, and other tools; and painting away with no lines or rules. Good for birthday parties or just a solo project, Lazy Daisy is an easy way to get handcrafted pottery you paint yourself.

1709 Monticello Rd., 434-295-7801

TIP

Studio fees are an affordable $11/day for adults, $9/day for children, but pieces range from $1 to $75, so be mindful of the price of the item you choose to paint.

BROWSE BEAUTIFUL BAUBLES AND FURNISHINGS
AT CONSIGNMENT HOUSE

Art. Antiques. Collectibles. Jewelry. Consignment House is our favorite place for a pre-dinner stroll. Drool over some vintage estate jewelry. Pine for a perfect piece of furniture to complement your home. A recent visit had us fascinated with a collection of vintage perfume atomizers on a tray, just the gift for the elegant woman who has everything. Eclectic art lines the walls and changes frequently. The jewelry selection is carefully curated. Gorgeous rings and pendant necklaces are there for your browsing and purchasing pleasure.

Local artist Randy Smith is frequently featured in the framed art that lines the walls. His Charlottesville cityscapes sell to residents and tourists looking to capture and take home the city's vibrant color and energy.

Other art includes antique and collectible pieces; they turn over often, and we make it a practice to stroll the store with some frequency so the next treasure to add to our home doesn't escape our notice.

121 W Main St., 434-977-5527
consignmenthousecville.com

SHOP FOR A CAUSE
AT MARTHA'S MARKET

Martha's Market features an excellent collection of vendor exhibitors from all over the country gathered for a single weekend each year. You pay a fee to shop this carefully curated collection, and it's all for a cause. Martha's Market, an annual event put on by the Martha Jefferson Hospital Foundation's Women's Committee to raise money for women's health, features over 70 unique boutiques with wares you won't find anywhere else. The Women's Committee has been successful in raising more than $4 million for outreach to women in underserved populations in areas such as breast health, midlife health, and heart disease.

shopmarthasmarket.com

TIP

Arrive at the market hungry enough to sample the wares of many food vendors, and expect to have most of your holiday shopping complete by the time you head home.

CHANGE YOUR LIFE WITH A BODY-POSITIVE SHOPPING EXPERIENCE
AT DERRIERE DE SOIE

Charlottesville's only independent lingerie shop is focused on helping its customers love their lingerie. The shop, owned by longtime bra fitter Megan Giltner, puts bra fitting first, knowing that a proper fit makes for the best customer experience. Bra fittings are complimentary, and the shop regularly stocks sizes from 30B to 44H.

Bras aren't it, though; the shop has a great selection of loungewear, sexy lingerie, and shapewear in a variety of sizes. The staff is willing and capable to advise those shopping for a gift as well.

Located on West Main, Derriere de Soie has its own off-street parking and is easy to find. A real departure from department store lingerie shopping, you owe yourself (or your friend, spouse, or partner) a body-positive lingerie shopping experience along with the power of a life-changing, well-fitting bra.

605 W Main St., 434-977-7455
derrieredesoie.com

ACTIVITIES
BY SEASON

There's always fun to be had in Charlottesville, but some events and activities are best enjoyed, or only happen, at specific times of year. Here are some ideas to keep you busy no matter the season:

ANYTIME

Dig Up a Literary Treasure at the University of Virginia Library, 98

Play Indoors at Virginia Discovery Museum, 108

Learn to Cook from Culinary Concepts AB, 6

Taste Locally Produced Spirits at Vitae Spirits Distillery, 8

Sip Your Tea at Twisted Branch Tea Bazaar, 24

Let There Be Light at Piedmont Virginia Community College, 94

Explore Black History at the Jefferson School African American Heritage Center, 95

Get an Artist's Education at the Fralin, 107

Earn a Master's in Manga at Telegraph, 116

Go Full Tilt at Decades Arcade, 42

Try Board Games with Local Connections, 40

SPRING

Watch Polo at King Family Vineyards, 61

WINTER

Cruise for Brews along the Brewery Trail, 7

Tour the Vineyards of Central Virginia, 10

• •

Take a Walk in the Dark on the Blue Ridge Tunnel Trail, 56
Play for Body and Mind at Wildrock, 69
Go Fish with Albemarle Angler, 85
Role-Play in Darden Towe Park, 83
Attend a History Dinner at Indigo House, 91

SUMMER

Float, Kayak, or Canoe on a River, 62
Pick Your Own Fruit from Local Orchards, 3
Take Off Early for a Free Concert at the Pavilion, 46
Go Up in the Air in a Hot Air Balloon, 60
Immerse Yourself in Art at IX Art Park, 41
Gaze at the Stars at Veritas Winery, 47
See a Tiny Concert in the Garage, 52
Try Gourmet Gelato in Splendora's Many Flavors, 4
Catch a Sunset at Sentara Martha Jefferson Hospital, 30
Visit a Tropical Oasis at Wood Ridge Farm Brewery, 22
Try a Paleta at La Flor Michoacana, 18

FALL

Sit on a Tractor Seat at the Top of Bear Den Mountain, 68
Bless the Hounds at Grace Episcopal Church, 99
Read Some Poe and See His Dorm Room at UVA, 93
Go Trick-or-Treating on the Lawn at UVA, 113
Make a Cheese Pilgrimage to the Monastery in White Hall, 2

· ·

SUGGESTED
ITINERARIES

MUSIC LOVERS

DATE NIGHT

SPORTS FANS

FESTIVALS

• •

THE GREAT OUTDOORS

Ride Your Bike through the Scenic Countryside, 63
Sit on a Tractor Seat at the Top of Bear Den Mountain, 68
Camp or Glamp in the Great Outdoors, 74
Take Your Dog for a Romp, 64
Visit Shenandoah National Park for Outdoor Adventure, 81
Gaze at the Stars at Veritas Winery, 47
Take a Walk in the Woods along the Appalachian Trail, 66
Go Fish with Albemarle Angler, 85
Row Your Boat on the Rivanna Reservoir, 72

FOODIE FAVORITES

Try Gourmet Gelato in Splendora's Many Flavors, 4
Be a Nachovore at Beer Run, 5
Attend a History Dinner at Indigo House, 91
Grease Your Spoon at the White Spot, 19
Sip Your Tea at Twisted Branch Tea Bazaar, 24
Try a Slice in a College Town, 16
Make a Cheese Pilgrimage to the Monastery in White Hall, 2
Find Out Why Bodo's is Where C'ville Buys Bagels, 14
Meet for Coffee at a Local Shop, 20
Satisfy Your Appetite at Dairy Market, 23

JUST OUT OF TOWN

Cruise Skyline Drive to See Stunning Views, 80
Experience Authentic Shakespeare at Blackfriars Playhouse, 50
Get Tubular with James River Runners, 86

• •

FUN WITH KIDS

OFF THE BEATEN PATH

• •

INDEX

Photo courtesy of Kate Duvall